Tall Grass And Trouble

A Story of Environmental Action

by Ann E. Sigford

Dillon Press, Inc.

©1978 by Dillon Press, Inc. All rights reserved
Second Printing 1981

Dillon Press, Inc., 500 South Third Street
Minneapolis, Minnesota 55415

Printed in the United States of America

Library of Congress Cataloging in Publication Data

Sigford, Ann E., 1950-
Tall grass and trouble.

Bibliography: p. 103
SUMMARY: Describes the vast grasslands of our continent as they were years ago, their eventual destruction, and the present efforts to restore them.

1. Landscape protection—Middle West—Juvenile literature. 2. Prairie ecology—Middle West—Juvenile literature. [1. Prairies. 2. Conservation of natural resources. 3. Prairie ecology. 4. Ecology] I. Title.
QH76.5.M53S53   333.7'0978   77-15560
ISBN 0-87518-153-8

CONTENTS

     Introduction   5
1. A Long Time Ago   7
2. The Natural Community   12
3. Fire and Ice—A Prairie Year   21
4. Who Eats Whom on the Prairie   34
5. Children of One Mother   44
6. The Prairie Meets the Plow   54
7. Once Lost, Forever Lost   64
8. A Patch of Weeds   70
9. Saving a Living History   75
10. Make Your Own Prairie   84
11. A Prairie National Park   91
     Notes   101
     Glossary   102
     Bibliography   103

These photographs are reproduced through the courtesy of Tim Anderson, photographer; Solomon D. Butcher Collection, Nebraska State Historical Society; Edward Curtis, *The North American Indian* (1907-1930) and the Minneapolis Public Library Athenaeum; David E. Johnson, photographer; the Kansas State Historical Society; Save the Tallgrass Prairie, Inc.; and the U.S. Fish and Wildlife Service: Donald Hammer, E. P. Haddon, Karl Maslowski, E. R. Kalmbach, W. P. Taylor, and Luther C. Goldman, photographers.

INTRODUCTION

The settlers who peeked through the last line of trees out onto the bright prairie meadows of Indiana and Illinois were woodsmen. Practiced in tree clearing and stump grubbing, they regarded the open land with suspicion. A common feeling was that land that couldn't grow trees couldn't be good for much.

It was a quiet land—bright and beautiful. The only sound one heard was the loud screech of the wooden wheels and the creaking of the wagons. Grass and flowers, bathed in sunlight, stretched over low hills to the horizon. Now and then a plump-bodied bird would rise up, hover for a moment, drop again, and disappear. The grass was full of hiding places for small creatures. Away from the wagons, smaller noises could be heard. A million grass blades, touching each other, whispered with the breeze.

The first pioneers who moved west followed the wooded river bottoms, and in the midst of fertile prairie expanses, they cut trees to make garden space.

Those who tried farming the grassland were discouraged, for the sod of matted grasses and roots was difficult to plow. Even if the farmers could cut through the sod, the sticky soil clung to the cast iron plows and had to be scraped off by hand every few feet.

Alert businessmen quickly set up "breaking companies" and, for a fee, would break a field using a giant plow pulled by eight or ten pairs of oxen.

The term "breaking" was apt. As the giant plow ripped through the earth, the bystanders heard loud popping and snapping noises as the centuries-old root systems were broken apart.

But once the tough roots rotted away, the finest soil in the world was ready for production; wheat, corn, and other grains and vegetables grew luxuriously. Many pioneers made their fortunes from the "useless" prairie soil.

Today, you and I cannot see what those settlers saw. The wild grasses and flowers have disappeared. Fields of grain are in their place. The prairie has been tamed to grow our food. From Ohio to Colorado and Canada to Texas, the prairie was plowed under wherever the plow could get at it. In other places it was grazed so heavily by cattle that it is almost unrecognizable as prairie.

But some small patches of prairie were spared, whether intentionally or not. Today, some people are trying to save and restore these bits of living history. In scattered places across the Midwest you can still find prairie. And if you use your imagination, you will still see that beautiful expanse that greeted the first pioneers.

1.

A LONG TIME AGO

Just as human immigrants traveled onto the prairie, plants and animals have also spread onto it whenever they could. Grassland has always been a land of opportunity, and, as we shall see, a land of hardship, too.

There has been a grassland in the middle of North America as long as the Rocky Mountains have stood. The Rockies started rising 25 million years ago. Eventually they were so tall that they interrupted the flow of wind that blows from west to east. The Rockies began snagging clouds, making them drop their moisture on the western slope of the mountains. The eastern side started drying up. Only by the time the clouds reached the Mississippi River did they scoop up enough moisture from the Gulf of Mexico to drop large quantities of rain.

The birth of a prairie after the Ice Age. At first, spruce trees line the rocky shores of a postglacial lake.

As the climate grows warmer, trees disappear and a prairie marsh is formed.

The damp forests that used to stand just east of the Rockies were replaced by an ancient, dry prairie. Animals adapted to life in a grassland soon took over the plains. There were rhinoceroses, giant pigs, horses with toes, large tigerlike cats, and many other strange creatures.

The old prairie passed away when the Ice Age began, about one million years ago. Great sheets of ice grew and then melted back several times.

Glaciers and cold weather displaced the plants and animals. Some kinds simply died out, while others survived farther south. When the most recent ice sheets melted back 12,000 years ago, the grassland plants and animals started to spread north again.

But the soil had been largely destroyed. In some places, only rock remained. Winds whipped up any exposed dust and swept it east, piling it 150 feet deep in many places.

Then the plants went to work soil building. First, they covered any dust and kept it from blowing away. They also sent their roots down and began pulling up minerals. If necessary, the roots even ground up rock so the minerals were easier to get at. When each generation of plants died, these minerals returned to the soil, in easy reach of other plants. The rotting plants became fertilizer for following generations. Where there was once bare dirt, there was now living topsoil.

It took a long time to make the rich topsoil that lay beneath the great prairie. As the climate changed, several different kinds of plants grew on the land and died away.

Richard Baker, a geologist, has studied the way the plants gave way to one another. Using a special hollow drill, Baker took out a core of mud from the bottom of Lake Okoboji in northwestern Iowa. This lake had been formed at the end of the Ice Age when a depression scooped out by the last glacier filled with melt water.

The mud core was eleven meters deep—as deep as a two-story house is tall. The deepest mud was the oldest. Baker examined it under a microscope and found preserved pollen grains from spruce trees and other plants that today grow only in the north. Spruce trees, well adapted to cool weather, must have grown in the shadow of the glacier. Some of their pollen blew down to the lake and was covered with mud. Other scientists have found the remains of musk oxen that date from the same period as far south as Iowa. This shaggy animal now lives only in the far north, along the shores of the Arctic Ocean.

The spruce trees and other cool weather plants started building soil on the shore of the lake. They prepared the ground for other plants. When Baker examined the mud a little higher in the core, he found that oak and elm tree pollen became more common while the spruce pollen decreased. Apparently, by 10,000 years ago, the weather had warmed up enough to melt the glaciers far away from Iowa. It was much too warm for spruces.

Checking farther up the mud core, Baker found only the pollen of prairie plants. In other words, it had grown too warm and dry even for trees. He estimates that Iowa has been prairie for 9,000 years.

The climate that leads to the development of prairies tends to create some survival problems for the plants and animals that live there. The prairie is hot in the summer and cold in the winter. It is windy and prone to wildfire and drought. There are no trees for shelter and little water for drinking. The only creatures that can live there have developed special survival techniques. In the following chapter we will look at the kinds of plants and animals that have "made it."

2.

THE NATURAL COMMUNITY

If you are from a woodland area, visiting a prairie can be like visiting a foreign country because the plants and animals are so unlike those you are used to. Even if you live in the prairie region, you have probably never seen an undisturbed prairie.

The prairie is different from every other natural community on earth. It has its own plants and animals that do not live in the woods or any other place. Most of them cannot live anywhere else. When the prairie was plowed, most of the living things had no place to go and are now very rare. In this chapter, we shall take a quick look at what plants and animals live in the prairie and how they have adapted to their homeland.

Prairie Plants

To learn about the prairie community, start with the plants. Unlike the animals, the plants are easy to see and do not move around. Also, certain plants are "indicators," or markers, of their community. If you learn to identify some of these indicator plants, you will be able to know a prairie when you see it. The other important thing about plants is that they are the foundation of the food web. They make the basic foods that all animals need from just sunlight, air, minerals, and water.

Grasses are different from other plants because of their skinny leaves and unusual tiny flowers. Many grasses are good prairie indicators. In fact, prairie is defined as "a natural North American grassland." Grassland has a character all its own. And even though plants cannot move, the grasses seem to set the prairie in motion.

There are about a hundred different kinds of grasses on the prairie. Some grow to reach over your head while others cannot reach the top of your shoes. There are grasses that grow in tight bunches, while others form a dense mat or sod.

The tall bunchgrasses like big bluestem and Indian grass grow where the soil is rich and moist, usually in the eastern prairies. They normally grow from waist to head high by late summer. Big bluestem and Indian grass indicate a "tallgrass prairie." In the drier west, though, in what we think of as the Great Plains, shorter grasses like buffalo grass and blue grama are indicators of "short grass prairie." They don't get much taller than your shoes. And between these extremes, are a variety of middle-size grasses like side-oats grama and sand dropseed.

Indian grass (left) is tall grass that prefers the moister ground of the eastern prairie. Short grass like blue grama (right) grows on the western plains.

Of course, a prairie is more than a field of wild grass—it must have flowers, too. In the early spring, even before the grasses are up, a number of beautiful flowers poke through and bloom very near the ground. By the time the grasses begin to claim the sunlight for themselves, the early flowers are finished for the year. But then other kinds of flowers, often in bright and beautiful colors, can take their turn. At any one time, the flowers in bloom seem to be about the same height as the growing grass. As the season goes on, taller flowers come into bloom. The reason is that flowers need sunlight to ripen their seeds. If they were shorter than their neighbors, they would be "shaded out" by the grass.

Puccoon (left) adds color to the June prairie. Later, butterfly weed (right) sports its orange flowers.

A side effect of the seasonal parade of flowers is that the prairie changes color every few weeks. Crex Meadows in Wisconsin is a good example. In early spring, most of the flowers there are pastel yellow and pink. But before long, flowers of bright orange, scarlet, and rich blue are blooming side by side. By fall, yellows and purples take over. After visiting a prairie over a season, many people think the woods are really drab.

What plants grow in a particular part of the prairie largely depends on the soil and climate. Once you know a few indicator plants, you can glance at a prairie and tell how dry it is and what the soil is like. After you have practiced for a while, you can even do it from a moving car, a skill which always amazes people who do not know about indicator plants.

The soil is the base of the prairie, while the plants that grow on it capture the energy of the sun and make it available to other living things. The plants are then food for everything from tiny insects to mighty buffalo.

Insects

Insects, because of their size and personality, are hard to take seriously. But remember, even though insects are little, there are a lot of them! Taken together, they have an enormous influence on all life on earth.

Insects are more obvious on the prairie than in the woods because they need sunlight for warmth. In the woods, most of them feed way above you in the tops of the trees. But in grassland, they are all over—in the ground, on the surface of the soil, and on every plant. Often, in the summer, you can sit quietly in the grass and actually hear the munching of thousands of tiny jaws and whirring of tiny wings.

Without insects, the prairie could not exist. For one thing, many of the plants need insects to pollinate them. Without bees, wasps, and butterflies to carry pollen from one blossom to another, prairie flowers could not make their seeds. These flowering plants, in turn, are food for many prairie animals.

Insects are also the great scavengers of the prairie. Beetles, wasps, and flies quickly take care of any animal carcasses left uneaten by larger creatures.

Those insects that eat grass are really tremendous grazers in spite of their small size. The grasshopper is the star of that department. Kansas alone has two hundred different kinds of grasshoppers in its prairies. In the old days, the grasshoppers alone ate so much that even the buffalo had to pay attention to them. Wherever the grasshoppers were common, they would eat so many plants that the buffalo would have to go somewhere else where there was more food to eat.

Other insects, like some beetles, dragonflies, and bugs, are predators. That is, they eat other insects and help to keep the prairie in balance.

Reptiles and Amphibians

Most people do not think of toads and frogs as typical prairie animals because they are associated with water. But many varieties live in the shallow ponds and marshes that are especially common in the eastern prairies. Others that need only occasional rain, like the spadefoot toads, live in the dry western prairies.

The toads and frogs are obvious only in the spring when they "sing" so loudly that you hear a slough or wet spot before you get close enough to see it. As tadpoles in the water, they act like fish. But as adults, they move onto land to capture insects and other small creatures. They are a link between the marsh and the upland prairie.

On the other hand, most reptiles are free from the requirement of needing open water and live on dry land. Some of the turtles are an exception. Snapping turtles, for example, leave the prairie slough only to lay eggs. Other prairie reptiles are active upland predators of insects, birds, amphibians, and mammals. Some of these are the bullsnake, hog-nosed snake, rattlesnake, and lizards like the prairie skink.

The little toad (left) is the most common amphibian of the prairie. Although the draining of prairie marshes has eliminated many shorebirds, an upland plover (right) can occasionally be seen. Large animals like the elk (bottom) are the ones most people associate with the prairie.

Mammals

Mammals have a great advantage over the amphibians and reptiles—their warm-bloodedness. Instead of relying on the sun for warmth, they can carry a warm climate around with them.

Like the insects, the mammals fill many roles on the prairie. The small plant eaters, such as the prairie dog, kangaroo rat, jackrabbit, and mouse, are a great link between the plants as producers and the predators. These little animals eat the plants and are, in turn, food for the meat-eating animals. The big-hoofed plant eaters, though, like the bison, pronghorn antelope, and elk, are the ones everybody thinks of as typical prairie animals. Bison, incidentally, are sometimes called buffalo, but bison is the correct term.

All of the plant eaters have their predators. The small animals are eaten by shrews, weasels, coyotes, and badgers. The rarest American mammal is the black-footed ferret, a predator of prairie dogs. Only the prairie wolf or plains grizzly bear could kill a bison, and then it had to be an animal that was weak or old. These large predators no longer roam the plains. When people began to farm the prairie, they killed off the wolves and bears they found there.

The role of scavenger is filled mainly by the striped skunk and the raccoon. Not usually considered prairie animals, they are as typical as the bison.

Birds

For such a harsh land, the prairie has a surprising variety of birds. They are most noticeable around wetlands. There, the ducks, geese, and little shorebirds can get the water plants and insects that they need to raise their broods of young. The young birds must grow fast enough to be able to migrate south before winter when the water is locked up as ice. Where the marshes have not been drained, these waterfowl still exist in large numbers. But the huge flocks of the past will never be seen again.

The upland birds, adapted to live on the dry prairie, are hard to find now that so much prairie has been plowed. Some, like the prairie chicken, were once common, and they provided tasty dinners for the settlers. Other birds, like the meadowlark, are still found singing along fence lines and hay fields. They have adapted to the lack of trees by nesting on the ground and perching on any tall object.

Meat-eating birds, like hawks and golden eagles, are essential to keep the rodents in check. And the scavenging vultures and magpies make sure that no carcasses are left for long.

The plants and animals that "made it" out on the prairie are beautiful examples of the way living things can adapt to their environment. Many of the prairie animals have relatives living in the woods that look quite different. The rodents that you think of as being typical of the woods—squirrels, beavers, and porcupines—are associated with trees. Prairie rodents, like the kangaroo rat and prairie dog, live underground and are associated with grass. Although they are all related, they live in very different areas and so are very different in shape and habits. In the next chapter, we shall see what problems prairie creatures must overcome and how they have done it.

3.

FIRE AND ICE— A PRAIRIE YEAR

If you visit a prairie on a summer day when it is pleasantly warm, the sky is lofty and blue, and the grass and flowers make a garden underfoot, you may become a fan for life. On a day like that, the prairie can be unbelievably beautiful. But go to the same prairie a month later, when there has been no rain, the temperature is in the nineties, and there is no shade in sight, and you might not be so impressed. That's when the prairie shows itself to be a tough and enduring land. I like it even better then.

In general, prairies exist where the summers are too hot, dry, and windy for forests. Droughts and their dust storms are a natural part of the prairie world. Prehistoric Indian villages were abandoned and covered with blown sand during ancient droughts. Early pioneers reported dust and sand blowing so hard that they could not see the trail.

In the 1930s drought again baked the prairie states. This time, though, the effects were even more dramatic than in past droughts because some of the land had been plowed. Whether killed by drought or plow, the dead vegetation could no longer hold the soil. It swirled in the streets of Chicago and even Washington, D.C. The Great Plains had become a huge "dust bowl." Those dusty days were nothing new for the prairie, and drought will, no doubt, come again. But you can be sure that the prairie plants and animals will fare better than our crops and we will.

How can the prairie organisms survive in what seems to us to be such a harsh place? It turns out that many of them could not exist in a "friendlier" climate. The prairie community exists where it does because all of the living things are well adapted to survive there, and they are able to repair the damage done by drought and dust storm.

Grasses, for example, have roots that are bigger than the rest of the plant. This is the opposite of a tree, which keeps most of its weight above the ground. The grasses drive down, even ten feet down, leaving just a little bit of the whole plant waving in the air. This is useful for surviving drought. If the roots probe deep enough, they will eventually hit some moisture. It is these deep roots, by the way, along with evaporation that brings minerals to the surface, that create the deep soil that made the prairie famous.

Not only do grass roots dig down, but also they reach across. One scientist dug up a chunk of prairie soil that measured three feet on each side and four inches deep and started picking out the grass roots. He estimated that the roots, when all pieced together end to end, would span twenty miles!

Other plants form large taproots in which to store water through dry spells. A teacher of prairie lore, David Costello, once told a student that when picking and pressing prairie plants for a collection, he should always include the roots. The student had no trouble until he decided to collect a specimen of the bush morning glory, a plant with beautiful pink flowers. After an afternoon of digging, he still had not gotten the root out, even though the hole he had dug was "large enough to hold a cookstove!" The bush morning glory root, at its largest, can be nearly two feet across. At three to five feet down, it branches out in different directions and may grow ten to fifteen feet deep. The root may weigh up to one hundred pounds.

Other plants solve their water problems in different ways. Some, called annuals, are around only when growing conditions are just right. They live a very short time, produce seed, and then die instead of trying to fight the weather. The embryo in the seed, protected by the seed coat, can usually endure until the next season's moisture. If necessary, some seeds will wait to sprout for years.

Prairie plants also have a special defense against the wind: they are short and flexible. A lone tree planted out on the prairie has a hard time surviving. The wind snaps twigs and leaves off. Windblown grit bruises the tender buds. Even the shaking itself damages the leaves. But in sheltered ravines and river bottoms, where the wind cannot reach them, trees can grow. For trees there is safety in numbers. That's why prairie settlers planted trees in clumps; each tree then helps to break the wind for its neighbors.

A lone tree has trouble surviving on the prairie. It wages a losing battle against the wind that sweeps across the empty plains with nothing to break its force.

Prairie animals are also equipped to endure heat, drought, and wind. The large ones, the bison and pronghorn antelope, have the great advantage of mobility. They can walk long distances to ponds and rivers for water and relief from heat. During the great droughts of the past, bison wandered east to the Appalachians and beyond, in their search for lush pastures. In the west, they even climbed the Rocky Mountains to find moisture.

Small prairie animals, since they cannot wander too far, have had to find other ways to avoid heat and drought. Two ways are by burrowing underground and being active only at night. The burrowing animals have special adaptations for digging. The badger's claws are two inches long, and even spadefoot toads have a hard, sharp-edged bump on the ankle of each hind leg to help them dig backwards into the soil. Burrows are a good refuge because they are much cooler and more humid than the ground surface. If it is very hot outside, a kangaroo rat's burrow may be twenty-five degrees cooler than the surface. Cool and comfortable, the kangaroo rat sleeps through the hot part of the day and comes out to get seeds in the nighttime coolness.

Seeds and juicy plants are good food choices for a small animal because there is water in them. Many prairie rodents get all the water they need from their food. Even the pronghorn antelope can live its entire life without ever drinking water. In addition, the pronghorns can eat most of the prickly plants that do well in dry times—even cactus, which they eat spines and all.

Perhaps the animals most affected by drought are the marsh creatures. During normal years, the ponds and marshes shrink in late summer, but the residents are prepared for this. The insects lay eggs for the next year, the turtles and toads dig into damp soil or mud, and the waterfowl fly to larger ponds. During bad droughts, marshes may dry up completely, but when moist weather returns, they will again teem with life.

How about your adaptations? If you go to visit a prairie on a hot summer day, you, too, will have to find a way to adapt to the climate. Burrowing is a little difficult, but at least you can wear a hat to shade your face and carry water to drink. If you are ever out there suffering in the heat, consider the creatures all around you that are especially adapted to survive out on the prairie.

When hot dry years descend on the prairie, the animals and plants can usually hunker down and endure. If the drought continues, some plants and animals may disappear from the area. Other, more desertlike species, finding a climate to their liking, gradually become more common. When the climate again swings to cooler and moister weather, the desertlike plants give way to lusher vegetation, possibly even trees. But for nine thousand years, the climate in the center of North America has favored prairie.

Fire goes hand in hand with hot, dry summers. For thousands of years, fires have sprung up suddenly around lightning strikes and spread from there across the prairie. Sometimes Indians set fires on purpose to send messages, drive bison, or invite their neighbors to move elsewhere. They also started some fires accidentally, as did later settlers. Until recently, there was nothing to stop one of these fires except rain or water in its path. It was not unusual for a single prairie fire to blacken two hundred square miles.

Even today, most wildfires occur in the spring and the fall when there is lots of dry grass lying around. If the

Fueled by the dried stalks and leaves of last summer's grass crop, a spring fire flares. A hot fire like this one burns quickly and moves on, leaving behind mineral-rich ash and growing room. Within a few days the prairie is green again.

day happens to be windy, fire can be terrifying. George Catlin, an early explorer and artist, after seeing a windblown fire in tall grass, wrote that the fire traveled so quickly that not even Indians riding their fastest horses could escape it. Forced to follow the zigzag paths of deer and bison through the thick grass, a horse and its rider would be overtaken by the thick column of smoke that was swept before the fire. The terrified horse would stand frozen with fear while the burning grass fell about it, in Catlin's words, "kindling up in a moment a thousand new fires, which are instantly wrapped in the swelling flood of smoke that is moving on like a black thundercloud, rolling on the earth, with its lightning's glare, and its thunder rumbling as it goes."[1]

These "fire blizzards" would kill any animal caught out in them, even bison. In 1804, a settler in southern Manitoba found a whole herd that had been burned to death by wildfire.

The Plains Indians, experienced as they were with the destructive power of fires, were skillful at avoiding them. Sitting Bull himself gave good advice to some Dakota schoolchildren in 1885—"Go to bare ground, or onto sand, gravel or plowing. . . . Go to a place with no grass. But do not run."[2]

Many prairie animals have their own survival tricks. Pronghorn antelope, for example, dash to high ground where the grass is sparse. The fire is less hot there, and they can jump over the fire line. After a fire, antelope can be seen eating cactuses and other juicy plants that do not burn well.

Burrowing animals simply retreat into their cool dens and let the fire pass overhead. Ground squirrels, mice, and kangaroo rats eat their stored seeds until the prairie

Both pronghorn antelope (top) and prairie dogs (bottom) are well able to cope with fire. The antelope runs away from it, while the prairie dog dives for its burrow.

greens up again. Pocket gophers eat roots anyway and are little affected. Scavengers, such as vultures, have a time of plenty—they eat the carcasses of animals killed by the fire. Predators such as coyotes and hawks still have their stock of rodents to eat. In fact, the rodents become especially easy to hunt as they explore the blackened ground. Birds fly to unburned areas. If their nests are destroyed, they usually wait a week or so and then nest again.

But what about the small animals that depend on green grass for food? If you ever have a chance to visit a prairie dog town, you will probably notice how prairie dogs keep their lawns mowed. They clip the grass around their burrows very short and keep it clear of litter and dead plants. Not only does this give them a clear view, but it leaves nothing for a fire to burn. The fire skips over the prairie dog town, and their food is unharmed.

Even where the plants have been burned to the ground, they will quickly reappear. The same root systems that protect against drought and cold also protect against fire because the heat penetrates only a very short way into the ground.

Long ago, the Indians noticed that the recovered prairie seemed greener after a fire than before. Burning removes the past year's dead leaves. We now know that if it is left to build up, this "litter," as it is called, will smother out the new shoots. As the fire burns the piled-up dead leaves, it turns them into ash, which is excellent fertilizer. So it is as if the prairie was mowed, raked, and fertilized by fire. Within a few days of a fire, most plants have sprouted again and grow with extra vigor. After a month has passed, you would hardly know that a fire had been there.

This is very different from the effect of fire in a forest. When trees are burned up to the top, they die, and it takes many years, even centuries, for trees to grow as tall again. Most prairie plants die down to the ground every year anyway, so a fire makes less difference. In the eastern prairies of Wisconsin, Ohio, Indiana, and Illinois, fire was often the main influence that kept the trees out.

Since prairie summers are hot, it is logical to assume that the winters would be mild. But this is not so at all. Just as summer dryness increases as you go west, winters grow more severe as you go north.

Cold winter winds streak across the plains and prairies, bringing stinging snow and ice. Sometimes sudden blizzards catch animals as well as people unaware. In about 1821, a "killer blizzard" in Alberta, Canada, piled up snow to a depth of fourteen feet. Thousands of bison and other animals died in the storm. Even fifty years later, the piles of skulls and other bones were testimony to the power of that one blizzard. People suffer, too. After a blizzard in Iowa in 1873, the surgeon at Fort Dodge amputated seventy human limbs that had been frozen in the severe cold.

Blizzards, of course, are extremes, but even normal winter weather calls for special adaptations on the part of the prairie plants and animals. Surprisingly, some of the adaptations that allow summer survival are the same as those that allow winter survival.

For example, deep root systems not only store water in summer, but they also serve as a reservoir of life in the winter. Snow insulates the ground from severe cold and keeps it from freezing too deeply. The roots can then lie dormant without freezing.

The seeds that are shed during the fall survive freezing

easily. In fact, some even need to be frozen before they will sprout. This requirement makes sure that they will not sprout during the fall only to be killed when winter comes.

Animals have their own set of defenses against winter cold. Many birds migrate to warmer places not so much because of the cold, but because their food supply has been cut off. A layer of ice, for example, separates waterfowl from the aquatic plants and animals they eat. Seed-eating birds, however, usually remain; seeds are good energy sources available throughout the winter.

Some prairie animals, such as the ground squirrel, avoid the problems by sleeping through it! Hibernation, of course, is much deeper than ordinary sleep. The animal's entire system slows down so that it seems nearly dead. Reptiles and amphibians have no choice but to hibernate. They cannot control their body temperature and will die if they freeze.

The hibernation habits of a common prairie amphibian turned out to be a key to understanding a puzzling prairie landform—the mima mound. Observers had long noticed that, even in stretches of prairie that were fairly flat, there were occasional mounds three or four feet high and perhaps ten feet across. They were covered with flowers and bushes that were not common to the rest of the prairie.

Many legends accounted for the mounds, but none made very much sense. Finally, a young scientist, John Tester, was studying toads near some mima mounds. He was trying to figure out how the toads spent the winter. People had assumed that they burrowed in the mud of ponds, but Tester proved that it was not so. He had sewn little radioactive pellets on the backs of toads and then found them again with a geiger counter. In late fall, he found the toads deep inside mima mounds—up to two thousand toads per mound! They had laboriously tunneled in during late fall to keep away from the freezing weather. Apparently, the mounds have been toad hibernation spots for thousands of years.

Unlike reptiles and amphibians, most prairie mammals do not hibernate. Some, like the black-tailed prairie dog, sleep through the worst weather, but most of the time they are active underground and live on food they have stored in their burrows. Others, like the coyote, grow a heavy coat of fur and hunt "by ear," as they listen for the sounds of mice and other rodents scrabbling under the snow. The snow serves as an insulating and windproof blanket that also hides the mice from view. Some small predators, like the shrews and weasels, find the mice's tunnels and catch their prey at home. On top of the snow, jackrabbits in their winter-white fur must stay constantly alert as they look for twigs and buds to eat, for the coyotes and owls are hungry, too. The largest prairie mammals, the bison, have few predators. Even so, the winter is hard on them. The only way they can get enough grass to eat is to use their huge heads as snowplows. Their long whiskers ice up and tear off at the skin. Sometimes, a bison trail will be speckled with blood from their muzzles.

Winter on the prairie is a hard time for plants and animals. In spring, the cycle of growth starts again, with only the toughest animals, those that lasted through the winter, as parents. While they work to raise their young, the dryness and heat slowly return, and a new set of survival problems must be faced.

Adapting to the climate is only the first step in survival. The vital issue of what to eat and how to get it is the next problem.

4.

WHO EATS WHOM ON THE PRAIRIE

All of us need to eat. Unlike you and me, though, many animals must spend most of their time just finding food and eating it. Almost all of the bisons' waking time is spent grazing. The reason is that they are plant eaters, and plants are a very bulky and inefficient fuel. But what about meat-eaters like the coyotes? Although they eat an energy-rich food, they must spend most of their time catching it.

Plant-eating animals, called herbivores, must have special "tools" to harvest their plants. If you have ever tried to yank out a tuft of grass and wound up with grass cuts, you understand the problem. Mice and rabbits use their self-sharpening front teeth as nippers. But some big herbivores, like the bison and pronghorns, have no top front teeth! Instead, they clamp the plants between their lower front teeth and the hard roof of their mouth and tear off with a shake of the head.

After being ground to a pulp by molar teeth, the plants can be digested into useful food. This takes a complex stomach and special bacteria. The bacteria live inside the bison's stomach and help digest the coarse fibers of the plants. Humans also have "friendly" bacteria in their digestive systems, but not nearly as many as the large herbivores. That is why people cannot live on grass like the bison.

Just as you and I have favorite and "unfavorite" foods, the prairie herbivores are very particular about what plants they eat. Some of them, like the bison and prairie dog, eat mostly grass and are called grazers. On the other hand, pronghorn antelope eat mostly bushes and plants other than grass. Pronghorns are browsers.

This selection of plants by herbivores has a great influence on the prairie. Suppose a large herd of bison ate most of the grass in one area. Then the flowers and bushes, which the bison do not eat, would get a chance to grow with little competition. But before the flowers would get too much of an advantage, the pronghorns, seeing a concentration of their favorite foods, would move in and eat many of them. Once again there would be a balance between grass and flowers. All the plant eaters together, large and small, help determine what plants will grow where on the prairie.

But with all these herbivores, why are there any plants left? You would think they would have eaten every last one. It turns out that the plants have a few tricks, too.

Some, like the cactus, have prickles and spines that discourage many herbivores from taking that first bite.

The flowers of the prickly pear cactus appear for only one day a year, but their nectar is irresistible to many insects. The plant itself is food for antelope.

But no defense is perfect, for the pronghorn eats cactus, spines and all. Other plants use chemical defenses like bad taste, smell, or even poison. After once tasting a particularly unpleasant plant, many animals, including people, will forever leave it alone. As usual in nature, though, one animal's poison is another animal's favorite dish. Many animals, for example, can eat poison ivy with no ill effects.

Even if all a plant's defenses fail, and it is eaten by an animal, all is not finished. Most herbivores eat only part of each plant and let the root remain untouched underground. The plant, after a short waiting period, just sprouts back. By that time, the animals will have moved on to a part of the prairie that has not been grazed over.

Grasses are especially resistant to grazing because each grass blade grows from near ground level instead of from high up on a stalk. It seems as if they get pushed up from the ground as fast as they are eaten. That is why you must mow your lawn so often in summer. But you had better not try mowing your flower garden!

As the bison and pronghorns and prairie dogs are chopping away at the leaves and stems, the seeds are falling away to the ground. Some of them are eaten by ants and birds, but many survive to grow next year's food. Some seeds, like the seeds in berries, need to be eaten before they will grow. They pass through the animal's digestive system unharmed and land on the ground complete with fertilizer to start new plants.

All in all, the herbivores and the plants they eat are in an endless tug of war on the prairie. Although the numbers of each kind change according to the situation, they have lived together for thousands of years.

How do the meat eaters fit into the scheme? They, of

The golden eagle's sharp eyes enable it to spot small animals on the ground while it soars in the sky above.

course, eat the herbivores as a way of life. The meat eaters, too, have special adaptations to allow them to catch and process the food they need.

First they need to find their prey out on the open prairie, where their meals can often see them coming a long way off. The coyote uses sharp eyes and ears and a keen nose to locate mice and rabbits. The golden eagle, soaring high on updrafts, has wonderful eyes that a human could match only with a good pair of binoculars. Good eyes are necessary to spot small animals in all that grass. The owl's eyes are further adapted to see well in the dark. In addition, the owl uses its ears to alert it to small rustlings. The rattlesnake uses heat detectors on its head to home in on the warm bodies of mice. It can also smell them since its forked tongue picks up the odors and pulls them into its mouth where it has special organs of smell.

Once the prey is detected, it must be caught. The speed

A coyote pauses at the entrance of its den, where dinner waits.

The jackrabbit's bulging eyes and long, mobile ears are as helpful as its powerful hindquarters are for staying out of danger.

of a diving prairie falcon leaves no time for a mouse to run away. The coyote, its tawny fur hidden against the grass, sneaks up as close as possible before dashing to the chase. And of course, all these predators are well equipped with killing tools of sharp teeth, talons, or beaks.

The ripping teeth of carnivores, as we call meat-eating mammals, are very different from the nipping and grinding teeth of the herbivores that they eat. Their stomachs are also very different. Instead of large, complex stomachs, the carnivores have fairly small, simple ones because meat can be digested more quickly.

Before you feel sorry for the small prey animals like

rabbits and mice, consider their defenses. For one thing, they tend to reproduce so fast there are always many survivors. In addition, most of them are sharp eyed so they can see their predators coming. Many of them, like the mice and jackrabbits, have bulging eyes that can see behind and above as well as ahead. And of course, they are camouflaged so they are difficult to see in the first place. Their hearing is sharp, too. A jackrabbit on the alert for danger will sit with one ear forward and one backward.

Beyond these alert senses, the herbivores have other methods of avoiding predators. One way is to sleep during the day, often underground, and to come out at night. Not only is it cooler then, but it is also harder to see. So many animals do this that the daytime prairie may seem lifeless to a casual visitor. At night, the skunks, mice, rabbits, badgers, coyotes, foxes, and owls are all out looking for food.

The prairie dog is one herbivore out during broad daylight. What is the reason for its courage? The prairie dog's chief defense is their social system. They live in huge "towns" with hundreds of burrows, many of which are interconnected. Each burrow entrance is surrounded by a mound of dirt that serves as both a flood barrier and a watch tower. All the residents keep watch for predators. When one is sighted, they whistle and bark a warning to all the others. If one "dog" is too far away from its own burrow, it uses someone else's. To make doubly sure no predators can sneak up on them, prairie dogs clip the grass and flowers into a wide lawn around the burrows. As well as serving as a firebreak, these lawns leave nothing for a predator to hide behind.

As effective as the defense of the prairie dog town is,

there is one predator specially adapted to capture them. The black-footed ferret is a kind of weasel that is so thin it can slip into burrows as fast as the prairie dogs can. The black-footed ferret is probably the rarest mammal in the United States. It became rare when ranchers and farmers poisoned the prairie dogs, whose towns were considered a nuisance. Many environmental groups are fighting to save some remaining towns in the hope that ferrets may appear to hunt their favorite prey.

The intricate system of the living prairie has been worked out over thousands of years. It needs no human help to operate, although humans can be part of it.

The sun is the driving force. It shines down and continuously energizes plants so they can take up water, gases, and minerals to create the basic food of everything else on earth. Plants are a way of combining the sun's energy with the earth's chemical elements. The other living things that eat them, from caterpillars to bison, use the plants as fuel for their own bodies. And when they in turn are eaten, they pass the fuel on to other creatures. Eventually, through death, decay, and animal waste, the chemical elements are returned to the earth, where the sun once more enables the plants to make use of them. This is true anywhere on earth.

How the cycle works in a given area—the ways in which climate, terrain, and soil determine what plants will grow and the ways in which other living things use the plants and one another for survival—is called an ecosystem. The last three chapters have described the ecosystem of the prairie.

In central North America, this ecosystem created a land of such beauty and riches that many people were attracted to it. Some of them became part of the ecosystem by receiving the sun's energy and the earth's substance and passing them on in the ageless manner. Small groups of American Indians, living in earthen or skin homes, hunting animals and gathering plants as necessary, were part of the prairie for many centuries. The prairie was different after they arrived, but it was still a diverse and beautiful grassland.

Unlike the Indians, the white settlers who later came to the prairie must have considered themselves not as part of the ecosystem, but rather as adventurers stumbling upon a treasure to be claimed. The hundreds of kinds of plants that had helped create the soil were quickly plowed under and replaced by a few preferred varieties. The insects and other small creatures found their original food sources destroyed and either died or adapted to the new crops. The settlers considered those that adapted to be their enemies and destroyed them. Large animals like bison were killed; some for food, and many for sport or to weaken the Indians.

The eastern tallgrass prairies, after thriving for nine thousand years, were nearly all plowed under in less than a century. The western shortgrass plains, although not plowed, suffered under continuous grazing by large numbers of cattle. Today there are only a few places where you can see the prairie ecosystem functioning at least partly as it did for so many years. These areas are precious —a glimpse of our history, a reminder of the great ages of the earth, a reminder of the fragility of life.

5.

CHILDREN OF ONE MOTHER

The people who first lived on the prairie felt a kinship with the other prairie creatures that seems incredible today. As Black Elk, a holy man and kinsman of Crazy Horse put it, the story of his people is the story of "us two-leggeds sharing in [life] with the four-leggeds and the wings of the air and all green things, for these are children of one mother and their father is one Spirit."[3]

Living on the prairie is a challenge for people as well as for plants and animals. There are few trees for building or fuel, little water, and a harsh climate. It is hard to find even a few good rocks for tools. Prairie plants adapt physically by growing deep roots. Prairie animals have the added advantage of being able to adapt their behavior. They may avoid the harsh winters by hibernating, or search for food at night to escape the summer heat. But unlike animals that follow set patterns of behavior set down by instinct, people adapt their way of life to each new situation. The way a group of people lives—what they eat, the houses they live in, the tools they use, and how they work and play together—is known as their culture. People can vary their culture to suit their surroundings.

When American Indians came to the prairie, they developed cultures well suited to the problems of grassland living. Since the prairie varies so much from east to west and north to south, different groups of Indians found different cultural solutions to their problems.

In the hot, dry shortgrass plains which stretch across the western portions of the Dakotas and Nebraska to eastern Montana and Colorado, crops are tricky to grow. The people who lived there had to rely on bison to provide them with food, shelter, and even tools. Success in hunting the huge animals was their key to survival. When the herds wandered over the prairie in search of forage, the people followed. Since the animals moved wherever and whenever they felt like it, the people could never build permanent villages. They spent their lives as wanderers, or nomads.

Imagine yourself as a plains nomad traveling on foot. How many of your favorite things could you carry with you? The Indians did train one common animal to help carry their possessions: the dog. The first white person to see the Plains Indians, the Spanish explorer Fransisco Coronado, wrote in 1541 that "They load the dogs like beasts of burden and make light pack-saddles for them like ours, cinching them with leather straps. . . . A load might be from thirty to fifty pounds, depending on the dog."[4]

Even so, there wasn't much room for bulky or breakable objects!

The nomadic Indians trimmed everything down to essentials but what they did own was doubly valued. Everything had its own carrying case so that it could be transported without damage. Even their beautiful feather headdresses could be packed into slim rawhide tubes.

The tipi was the shelter of the plains nomad, and for good reason. It was light, easy to pack, beautiful, and comfortable. A tipi could be set up in twenty minutes and taken down in five. The long poles that supported it were lashed together to make a travois that could be loaded with belongings and hitched to a dog. An entire camp could be on the move within half an hour. As Standing Bear, an Oglala Sioux, described it, the tipi was a comfortable shelter indeed:

> In case of rain, both flaps were closed down and tied to a stake driven into the ground. . . . There was never any smoke inside, as the flue was open at the top. If snow fell heavily, it banked up all around the tipi, which helped keep us warm. On nights when there was a cold, sleeting rain, it was very pleasant to lie in bed and listen to the storm beating on the sides of the tipi. It even put us to sleep.[5]

The tipi was truly a classic mobile home, and the point of all this mobility was to be able to pursue the bison.

Killing a powerful animal such as a bison, which stood six feet at the shoulder, could not have been easy. Imagine hunting them on foot in a treeless area with nothing more powerful than a bow for a weapon! But a skilled hunter could kill a bison with one well-aimed shot, and the nomadic Indians invented several clever hunting techniques. Since wolves constantly traveled with the herds in hopes of picking off a weakened animal, the bison

The tipi of the plains nomads was the first American mobile home.

were used to them. A hunter disguised as a wolf could get close enough to the animals to shoot at them. Hunters also hid themselves in brush blinds at watering places.

To kill many bison, however, the hunters had to use a trap of some kind. In some places, bison could be stampeded over a cliff. Unfortunately, the prairie is not known for having a lot of cliffs! Sometimes ravines could be used. And sometimes the only way to trap a herd was to build a strong semicircular corral on the side of a hill. The logs forming the sides were pointed and poking into the enclosure. The bison would be stampeded over the hill only to find themselves caught in a spiky pen with people shooting arrows at them.

Having gotten food to eat, the next problem was how to cook it. What little wood there was, was too precious to burn. So the bison helped out again; the primary fuel was dried bison droppings (buffalo chips). The nomads also burned grass by twisting bunches of it into tight bunches.

If everything worked right, many bison, sometimes more than could be used, were killed all at once. An immediate problem was preventing spoilage of the tons of meat lying in the sun.

The activity on the plains must have been frantic as the women skinned, butchered, and cut up the meat. Most of the meat was cut into thin strips and hung up to dry. An early European explorer, who was with a group of nomads after a great hunt, saw strips "hung up by the hundreds and thousands of poles resting on crotches, out of the reach of dogs or wolves, and exposed to the rays of the sun for several days. It becomes so dry it can be carried to any part of the world without damage."[6]

Jerky, as the dried meat was called, could be eaten as

it was, but it tasted better stewed. To make pemmican, jerky was roasted and then pounded and mixed with tart berries and fresh animal fat. Packed in flat rawhide boxes, pemmican would last for a long time, even in summer.

During the butchering of the bison, nearly all parts were used for something. The bison were a supermarket, hardware store, and clothes shop all in one. Sinews could be made into bowstrings and horns into cups. The hides were sewn together for tipis, and thick pelts made warm robes for winter. No wonder the Blackfeet called the bison *Ni-ai,* which means "my shelter and my protection."

In a hundred ways, the nomadic Indians adapted their customs to survive out on the shortgrass plains. East of them, in the tallgrass prairies, other Indians developed a different way of life based on farming.

The farming Indians of the eastern grasslands built prosperous villages wherever corn, their staple crop, would grow. These villages were nearly always located in river valleys where water and some trees were available and where the soft soil was easy to till with a simple stone or bone hoe.

These Indians, like the nomads, developed houses that used very little wood. The Pawnees of Kansas and Nebraska, for example, lived in circular earth lodges that were large enough to house ten to twenty people. Sturdy wooden posts cut from the large trees that grew in the river valleys held up the domed earth roof. A tunnel-like entryway kept cold winds out, and a fireplace in the center made the lodge warm in winter.

Other people used grass or reeds to build their houses. In Missouri, where the winters were not so severe as farther north, the Osages lived in long domed houses of poles covered with rush mats. Each house was large enough for several families. Other tribes used small thatched houses. None of these dwellings used much wood, but they still offered the necessary protection.

In most farming tribes, women were in charge of growing food. They planted several crops, but the most important was corn. Corn is a special kind of grass introduced into North America from Mexico almost two thousand years ago. The original corn from Mexico was a lush tropical plant that took five months to mature. Over the centuries, the farming Indians converted it into a tough, hardy, reliable crop that was ready to eat in a little more than two months. Modern scientists have called their feat a "great achievement in plant breeding." Today we still use corn varieties originally developed by the Indians, but some of their corn grew without irrigation in places where none of the modern strains will!

Most of the Indian varieties of corn were quite small, and the ears were red, blue, or white as well as yellow. The Indians ate their fresh corn roasted or boiled and dried the rest of the crop for later use. Then it was made into mush or soup and mixed with other foods.

The Indians also raised beans, squash, tobacco, and sunflowers. Like corn, these crops had never been used by the whites before they were obtained from the Indians. The great northern bean, for instance, often used to make baked beans, is the descendant of a handful of seeds given to Oscar H. Will by Son of Star, a Hidatsa Indian.

Although the farming Indians took advantage of the deer, raccoons, and wild turkeys that lived in the sheltered valleys near their villages and the fish and clams in the nearby rivers, their chief big game animal was also the bison.

The Witchita Indians of Kansas and Nebraska were farmers who lived in villages. Because of the shortage of wood, they built their homes of grass. Some of these grass lodges were as large as thirty feet across.

Since bison were often found far from the villages, most farming groups had to pack up and roam until they got the meat they needed. On these hunting trips, they used tipis and dogs much like the nomads to the west. The big hunts usually took place in the spring after the gardens were planted, and sometimes in early winter, after the harvest.

The Plains Indians, both farmer and nomad, were constantly aware that they were able to survive only because of the creatures with whom they shared the prairie. Killing a first animal, for example, was a major event in a young boy's life. It marked a dividing line between being dependent on everyone else and being a provider who helped the tribe. Standing Bear tells what happened when he brought his first bird back to camp. "My father was so happy. . . . He notified the camp crier to announce that his son had killed his first bird, and that his father was giving away a horse in consequence. On this occasion the horse was given to an old man who was very poor. . . . This was the beginning of my religious training."[7]

During this training, children learned that animals, like humans, had souls and, like humans, deserved reverence. The Teton Sioux had religious ceremonies to insure that the bison herds would continue in spite of hunting and asked pardon of their spirits for killing them. They believed that if the hunters were wasteful, the bison would leave and the people would starve.

The Indians did not feel that they were making a living off the prairie; rather, they were part of it. The earth was the living mother of all things, and the grass of the prairie was her hair. No wonder they were so outraged by the customs of the whites, who thought in terms of land to be used, bought, and sold. Smohalla, a Nez Percé, replying to a white demand that his people move to a reservation and live like the whites, said, "You ask me to cut grass and make hay and sell it, and be rich like the white man. But how dare I cut off my mother's hair? It is a bad law, and my people cannot obey it."[8]

The Indians were part of the prairie for several thousand years. No one knows what it would have been like without them. They certainly affected it by gathering plants, killing animals, digging in the soil, and starting fires. But compared with the invasion of white settlers to come, their presence was lightly felt. One reason is that when their population reached its peak around 1800, there were only about two hundred thousand Indians scattered over the vast plains. The prairie cannot support many more people than that. It took the construction of railroad lifelines to the east and west before the number of white invaders could increase. The prairie settlers had to import metal tools, lumber, glass, farm animals, garden seeds, and many other things in order to live.

With a communication and supply network to support them, plus a philosophy of farming wild land, the settlers quickly changed the face of the prairie. It has only been recently that some of the descendants of these settlers, seeing the results of so much destruction, were attracted to the Indian belief that we are all children of the earth.

6.

THE PRAIRIE MEETS THE PLOW

In the early 1500s, a new people arrived on the prairie. The Spaniards, after conquering the Aztec Indian empire of Mexico and plundering its wealth, started exploring to the north and east and reached the heart of the prairies by 1541. The Spanish explorers were looking for more gold, but they did not find any on the prairie. They did find Indians, whom they treated as a natural resource to be used like the land.

The Indians learned about guns from the Spanish and about the horse, an animal that had not been seen on the prairie for thousands of years. Guns and horses obtained in skirmishes with the Spanish were quickly traded throughout the western plains. At the same time, the whites were settling the eastern seaboard. The eastern

Indians, who had at first welcomed the whites, were now homeless. Armed with captured guns, they looked to the west for new homes, but found only land already claimed by other Indian groups. Desperate wars broke out as the people fought for a place to live.

By 1700, the Sioux, who had originally lived in the eastern woodlands, had been pushed as far west as central Minnesota. Armed with guns and fighting all the way, they crossed the Missouri onto the plains in 1725. Once on the plains, they soon acquired horses. By 1800 the Sioux were the masters of North and South Dakota, having been converted from woodland farmers to mounted buffalo hunters in one lifetime. It happened all over the prairies. Forced out of their eastern homelands, the Crow, the Cheyenne, and the Plains Chippewa tried making it out on the prairie.

The ones who really lost out were the original farming Indians of the eastern prairies. The peaceable and prosperous Mandan of the upper Missouri are a sad example. In 1795, Trudeau wrote that there had been several "populous villages, now depopulated and almost entirely destroyed by the smallpox which has broken out among them three different times."[9] By 1804, the seven Mandan villages were reduced to two poor ones. In 1837 one smallpox case on the steamboat *Assiniboin* spread and wiped out nearly all the rest. The few survivors joined other displaced farming tribes, but their new village was destroyed by hungry Sioux fighting their way west. The last earth lodge town built by the Mandans on the Missouri is now beneath the waters of the Garrison diversion project.

The Indians who adopted the horse and gun had the advantage, at least for a while. On the prairies, the horse

A warrior and his horse stop by a prairie pool for a drink in this photograph taken around 1900. By that time the bison had left the plains.

meant freedom of travel. Instead of walking fifteen miles in a day, they could ride sixty. Instead of hoping the bison would wander close to their traps, they could go out and get them. Instead of walking for days to reach a village they wanted to raid, they could strike out in one night. And the gun, of course, gave a great advantage in warfare and hunting. The plains were in a turmoil.

The turmoil lasted only as long as the bison lasted, which was not long at all. By 1880, bison herds that had once numbered 60 to 75 million animals had been greatly reduced by wasteful hunting. Some whites killed them for sport or for the purpose of destroying the Indians' food supply. In 1907, fifteen bison had to be shipped from the New York Zoo to stock the nation's first bison refuge near Cache, Oklahoma. The old way of life was gone forever.

Most whites had such a poor opinion of the prairie that they could not understand how anyone could live there at all. A famous anthropologist of the day, Lewis Morgan, wrote in 1859 that "the prairie is not congenial to the Indians, and is only made tolerable to him by possession of the horse and rifle."[10] Wouldn't the past generations of hunters and farmers have been amused!

The early explorers were especially disappointed that they did not find lush forests over all of their New World. Their disappointment is reflected in some of the early maps of the prairie. Perrin du Lac's map of 1802 indicates most of Nebraska as "a great desert of moving sand where there is neither timber nor soil nor rock nor water nor animals except some small varicolored tortoises."[11] The sand hills of Nebraska are dry, all right, but not that dry! Even the much moister prairies of Minnesota were described by William Stewart in 1838 as "an utter desert."

Some of the early explorers liked the grasslands. Joseph Nicollet's exploring party, crossing the same land just described as utter desert, enjoyed "a lovely day and the coolness that accompanies us on the ravishingly beautiful rolling prairie that we cross."[12] And George Catlin, a famous artist of the West, painted a picture with words as he described the prairie at sunset, "when the green hill-tops are turned into gold—and their long shadows of melancholy are thrown over the valley—when all the breathings of day are hushed and nought but the soft notes of retiring dove can be heard; or the still softer and more plaintive notes of the wolf, who sneaks through these scenes of enchantment."[13]

Even while noting the beauty of the prairies, most explorers doubted its fertility. The first white settlers farmed in the timbered river valleys just as the Indians did. Not only were there trees, which was a good sign, but the soil was easier to till, too.

There was another thing about the valleys that they liked—it reminded them of their homes back east or in Europe. As late as 1867, timbered valley land in Iowa sold for thirty to fifty dollars per acre while upland prairie was nearly given away for three to ten dollars per acre.

The prairies were frightening. People were actually lost more quickly out there than in heavy forest. There just did not seem to be any landmarks, except to the Indian. Many were homesick for trees and villages as they had known them before. As one pioneer cried, "How will human beings be able to endure this place? Why, there isn't even a thing that one can hide behind!"[14]

Many of the people had no choice but to stay. They had used up the last of their money just getting out there.

Since wood was in such short supply, the early settlers, like the nomads, had to gather buffalo chips for their fires.

And for many of them, it was their only chance to own land. The East was already crowded and the land expensive, so they stayed. As a settler's joke put it, living on the prairie was "a lot like getting hanged: the initial shock is a bit abrupt but once you hang there for a while you sort of get used to it."[15]

Living in such an open place required a good shelter, but traditional wood homes were out of the question. Like the Indians, the settlers turned to the soil for building. They used a special "grasshopper plow" with a horizontal blade that could peel off a strip of sod eighteen inches wide and three or four inches thick. These were cut into oblong "bricks" about two feet long, and stacked to make the thick walls of a sod house.

The insides of most sod houses were dark and dirty, almost like a cave. But a dark retreat was exactly what most people wanted after a day in the sun. The soddies were a real shelter from cold, heat, and wind. Even fires would pass by without burning one up. But there were problems, too. As one pioneer folksong puts it,

> The roof has no pitch,
> it is level and plain,
> But I never get wet —
> unless it happens to rain.[16]

Rainwater would soak into the sod and drip for days after a storm.

Once the settlers had built their shelter, the work of farming began. Plowing was difficult, to say the least. The cast iron plow that had worked perfectly well back home could not get through the tangle of roots that bound the topsoil together. If it did penetrate the roots, the rich soil stuck to the wooden mouldboard and would not flip over, or "scour." With a great deal of work, a

(Top) Getting ready to build a prairie home, settlers load strips of sod on their wagon. (Bottom) A sod house in Nebraska. Note how every bit of land is being used to grow corn.

settler could plow some land, but progress was so slow that one could starve before enough land was plowed to live on. Some newcomers survived by planting "settler" corn. They struck the sod with an ax, dropped some seeds in, and hoped for some kind of a crop. Meanwhile, they plowed, and plowed, and plowed.

If a family still had some money left, they could hire a "breaking company" to get the fields ready for planting. These companies used huge, wheeled plows pulled by as many as six yokes of oxen. To the settler's horror, the breaking companies could charge whatever they wanted for the service. At $12.25 per acre, it often cost more to plow the land than it did to buy it!

By 1840, all this changed. John Deere invented a steel plow that was strong and tough and had such a smooth mouldboard that the soil wouldn't stick to it. Virgin, or unplowed, prairie became more and more rare.

Farming put an end to the prairie as it used to be. Most of the wild plants would no longer grow except where land was left unplowed. The wild animals that depended on the plants either adapted to the new crops or became rare, if not extinct.

Other changes were more subtle. By plowing, the settlers created firebreaks. In the eastern prairies, trees could then invade areas where they had been previously kept out by fire. Settlers planted trees, too, as windbreaks that have greatly changed the overall look of the grasslands.

Many new plants came west with the settlers. The crops, of course, were brought on purpose to replace the prairie plants. But uninvited guests, hidden in the mud on boots and plows and mixed in with crop seed, came along for the ride. Today these European weeds are the most common plants other than crops in most of the prairie states. They include such lawn and garden pests as dandelions, most thistles, lambs quarters, plantain, and quack grass. If a piece of virgin prairie is disturbed ever so slightly, these bold European weeds may dig in and change the makeup of the land.

Unlike the bison that left an area after they had grazed on it for a while, the cattle were confined by fences. Then, if the rancher was not careful, the plains could be overgrazed so severely that the original plants would be wiped out as surely as if they had been plowed under.

When the prairies were either plowed or overgrazed, erosion soon followed. The scary thing about erosion is that, once lost, soil is really lost. If it is swept away by the wind, it usually winds up someplace where it is not desirable, such as on your windowsill at home or in the ocean. It would do a lot more good out in the plains where it was formed!

Of course, soils can be rebuilt, but the process is slow; it took prairie plants several thousand years. Today with fertilizer, even poor soils can be farmed, but soil lacking old-fashioned rotted plant matter cannot hold its moisture. The land becomes especially susceptible to drought and more erosion.

What we are talking about here is even more terrible than the destruction of the plant and animal community. Soil is the basis of the whole ecosystem—if we squander that, it will destroy us. As John Madson puts it, "spending is one thing; bankruptcy is another."[17]

7.

ONCE LOST, FOREVER LOST

When prairie plants are destroyed, animals are bound to get hurt, too. Sometimes the danger comes and goes so quietly that few people notice. Jim Zimmerman, of the University of Wisconsin arboretum, is one who notices and cares, too. Thirty years ago, he started observing a rare prairie flower; the green milkweed. He could find only three clumps of the plant in the entire state of Wisconsin, and he discovered something strange and frightening. Although they flower well, they have not produced seeds once in those thirty years. Zimmerman even tried pollinating the flowers by hand, but still no seed. His conclusion is that some kind of tiny bee, the only one that pollinated that flower, became extinct before anyone even knew it existed. Even if the green milkweeds that are now alive are able to survive for years to come, they are the end of a line that has spanned thousands of years. It makes you wonder how many other plants and animals you and I will never have a chance to see.

Some animals, like the bison, have had a narrow escape from extinction. By 1889, 551 bison remained from the many millions that had roamed the plains forty years earlier. People began to fear that this animal, native only to the North American plains, would soon be lost altogether. Game laws were passed and other efforts were made to help the bison that were left survive and reproduce. Their concern paid off. Today about fifteen thousand bison live in game preserves in the Black Hills and the Badlands of the Dakotas. A few more roam wild in our national parks, and some ranchers raise others for meat.

Many prairie birds that used to be common are also rare or extinct now. Golden plovers once spread over the prairie in great flocks during migration. On March 16, 1821, John Audubon watched hunters near New Orleans shoot 48,000 golden plovers in one day as they tried to fly north. The hunters had what seemed to be an endless supply of birds, but today they are very rare. The prairie chicken has shared the fate of the golden plovers. David Costello's grandfather once told him that in the 1870s one shot across his corncrib would kill enough prairie chickens to furnish a meal for his family of eight. There were so many prairie chickens in Minnesota that they were bundled into barrels and shipped to Chicago for hog feed!

Other creatures of the prairie, such as the black-tailed prairie dog, are just now becoming scarce. This large rodent lives in large "towns" in the shortgrass plains.

A male prairie chicken performing his spring mating dance. He dances to his own drum: the orange sacks on his throat fill with air to help create a booming sound.

Ranchers dislike prairie dogs not only because their burrows trip cattle and horses, but also because they eat grass that ranchers feel should belong to cattle. The prairie dogs, however, do not take much grass from cattle since they actually prefer closely grazed land. Prairie dogs greatly increase in numbers where previously healthy land has been overgrazed by cattle or sheep. Unfortunately, they are blamed for the overgrazing. Today, after being shot, trapped, and poisoned, they exist mostly in refuges such as Wind Cave National Park in the Black Hills.

David Costello saw what happened to one prairie dog town after most of its residents had been killed by poison. A normal town is divided into many separate "clans."

The members of a clan cooperate with one another in digging burrows, watching for enemies and so on, but are unfriendly with other clans. In Costello's town, the survivors were from widely separated clans and did not know one another, so they did not cooperate. The thousand pair of eyes that used to watch for enemies were reduced to a few. "In the second summer after the poisoning, wheatgrasses, pigweeds and other tall plants grew faster than the prairie dogs could clip them down for good visibility," Costello reported. "At last, only one prairie dog remained. I saw it sitting lonesomely on its mound in the late summer of 1949. I suspect that a coyote or a golden eagle ended its existence."[18]

The scarcity of the prairie dog has brought about the scarcity of other creatures that depend on it in one way or another. There is a small owl, for example, that beats the heat by living underground in abandoned prairie dog burrows. Since the burrowing owls cannot dig their own holes, they need the prairie dogs to do it for them. So they have become rare, too.

The black-footed ferret, which is the main predator of the prairie dog, is now one of the world's rarest mammals, thanks to the loss of its food supply. Few people have ever seen one. One of those who has, describes the ferrets as "extremely beautiful little animals. They are small—no bigger than a mink. Their round heads, large round ears that stand out alertly, inquisitive shoe-button eyes surrounded by the mask of black fur, and black noses give them a face that is utterly beguiling."[19]

The ferret lives among its prey; it even uses a modified prairie dog burrow as a den. When a ferret moves in, neighboring prairie dogs rush over and plug the hole as to trap the ferret inside. But the ferret is an excellent

A rare photo of a rare animal. The black-footed ferret faces extinction.

digger, too, and just digs itself out whenever it chooses.

It would seem that the ferret lives like "a robber baron securely established in the village of his helpless peasantry,"[20] as one writer declared in 1929. But a prairie dog weighs every bit as much as a ferret, and it is not exactly a pushover. Observers have seen prairie dogs chase a ferret and even win a fight with one. Apparently, the reason why a ferret hunts at night is that the prairie dogs are sleeping and may be caught unaware.

Ferrets have been rare for many years. As long ago as 1896, when a government scientist tried to study them, he could find only six of them, and those six were skins in museums! Maybe they were always uncommon. If we could study them more, we might be able to find out why. But the ferret is at the very point of extinction today.

Saving the ferret is going to be difficult. One reason is that few citizens are even aware that there is such a little animal and that it is in danger. The Fish and Wildlife Service receives many more complaints about prairie dogs than letters asking them to save ferrets. The service has, however, paid ranchers two dollars an acre per year for saving as many acres of prairie dog town as they have. If ferrets live in those towns, they are safe for the time being. It has also been suggested that large refuges be set up in the few places where ferrets still exist. But it is hard to prove that ferrets live in any one place. They are shy animals that hunt at night and stay underground most of the time. A third, and very risky, answer to the problem is to capture several ferrets and breed them in a special research center. If the ferrets do not choose to breed, however, these rare captives may die for nothing.

So much has already been lost that it is hard to believe we can lose still more. And yet every day prairies are being plowed, and prairie marshes are being drained. In some places, virgin prairies are actually built over; the sod is removed and replaced with European bluegrass and houses. The people who move there may have no idea of the destruction that went on before their homes were built.

Today tallgrass prairie is the rarest of the prairie types. The only sizable tract of tall grass left is in the Flint Hills of Kansas. Since the prairie there is underlain by rock, the soil is too shallow to plow. For years it had been preserved because no one wanted it, but now people are trying to save it as a park.

8.

A PATCH OF WEEDS

I have noticed that once you become interested in the prairie and start talking about it with people, they smile and think it is just fine that you have such a strange hobby. But sooner or later they will be put on the spot. Maybe the preservation of a prairie will affect them by increasing their taxes. Then they may be a lot more skeptical. "Why save a patch of 'weeds'?" they may ask. Then you really have to think.

   Those who belong to The Nature Conservancy, a group devoted to preserving wild lands, have thought about this question for some time. Their answer is that the most important reason for preservation is to keep up the natural diversity of our world. They want to preserve representatives of every major kind of ecosystem in the country.

Because large tracts of tall grass are rare, the chance to walk through a stand of big bluestem is an opportunity few of us have.

Just think for a moment of the natural diversity that can be found within our national borders. The United States has beaches, mountains, marshes, deserts, forests of several kinds, and even now—prairies. But in the last one hundred years the land has grown less diverse. Forests have been cleared and farmed, prairies have been plowed, and marshes have been drained. Clearing, farming, and building have so changed the contour and nature of the land that sometimes it is hard to tell what it once was. Our human influence has made it all look the same. This is the loss of diversity, and it frightens many people.

One reason they are afraid of losing diversity is that a simplified habitat is biologically unstable. (A habitat is the place where a plant or animal lives, and the features of that habitat limit the kinds of living things that can survive there.) A prairie habitat might be able to support 250 species of plants, 100 species of birds, and 50 species of mammals. If a disease appeared that would hurt one kind of plant, the overall system would not be destroyed because there would be 249 other plant species that might be able to take its place until the disease had run its course. The animals that ate the plant might be able to rely on another kind. But let's say you plow the prairie, thereby eliminating all the wild plants, and replace them with one plant—corn. You eliminate all the wild animals and replace them with one animal—humans. What would be the effect of a disease that wipes out corn? The plant cover lies dead, the soil is exposed to the gnawing of the wind, and the people are without food. Farmland, because it is a simplified habitat, is apt to be unstable.

In the 1930s, dry weather killed thousands of acres of food crops. The soil blew away and may never be rebuilt. Where there were healthy bits of prairie, though, the plants that could not bear the drought went dormant, while drought-resistant species increased. Some of the few places that kept their soil intact were unplowed prairies.

Thus, one practical reason we should save some prairie is to make sure we have some healthy land left. As a Nature Conservancy newsletter put it, "If we ignore the ecological facts of life and really try to act as if we had 'conquered' nature, sooner or later nature will get even, because no human is that smart."[21]

Only by preserving the original prairie, can we gauge what is happening to the farmland we have made from the rest. By comparing the topsoil in virgin prairie remnants with the plowed land next to it, a study has concluded that "the United States has lost one-fourth of its top soil since the prairies were first broken by the plough."[22] If the prairie could not be used as a baseline, there would be no way to measure the loss. As John Madson puts it, "We'd never dream of melting down the platinum meter in Paris and converting it to jewelry; it is the master rule, an original measurement upon which so much engineering and science are based. And so, in an even greater sense, is native prairie."[23]

Another reason to keep a good selection of diverse wild land is that you never know what plant or animal might prove useful in the future. The United States Department of Agriculture has a special unit, the Medicinal Plant Resources Laboratory, that attempts to identify new, useful plant substances. Sometimes the useful substances come from rare plants. For example, a drug that may help in cancer treatment was obtained from a shrub that was growing in Ethiopia. The shrub could not produce the drug in quantity, however, and the experimenters started looking for a better source. They found it in a related shrub that was so rare it grew only in a forest preserve in South Africa. A few years ago, no one would have missed the plant if it had become extinct, but now many cancer sufferers are grateful that it was preserved.

A desert bush in Arizona recently made headlines when it was discovered that an oil made from it could be substituted for sperm whale oil. It may turn out that the sperm whale will be saved because of a bush in the desert. Who knows what future discoveries will be made about wild prairie plants? It seems unwise to let any living thing become extinct when we are just starting to learn about the natural world.

A fourth reason to preserve the diversity of the prairie is for the delight it gives people. No one drives to a cornfield to have a picnic! Nearly every place that people think is beautiful has diversity. The prairie, with its changing colors, shadows, and sounds is beautiful because it is rich in diversity.

Perhaps the most important reason to preserve prairie and other natural areas is that we have a responsibility as part of the community of the earth not to harm the other parts. It is such a terrible power that we have. If we cause something to become extinct in our lifetime, it will change the world for people in the future. Their world will be missing something, and it will have been our fault. Who has the right to make such a final decision?

9.

SAVING A LIVING HISTORY

Concern over loss of the prairies and their wildlife is not new. In 1844, some settlers in Illinois wrote, "We have made several attempts, heretofore, to transplant the wild flowers from our beautiful prairies, into our garden, to preserve and domesticate. . . . A few years will deprive us of these beautiful flowers in their wild state, and unless they are domesticated, the next generation will not know what they were."[24] In the past, few people shared this concern. But in the last twenty years, more and more people have been trying to do something about the loss of prairie.

One of the groups that has been the most active in prairie preservation is The Nature Conservancy (TNC). The Nature Conservancy has been saving land since

1951, long before it was fashionable to be concerned about the environment.

TNC is a nonprofit corporation controlled by its members. The advantage of forming a corporation is that as long as it has the money, it can buy land quickly, just as an individual can. The government, on the other hand, is slowed down by following regulations that make sure that a piece of land is just right, that everyone knows about the sale, and that the price is fair. All too often, the price rises as soon as the owners know that the government is interested.

TNC, on the other hand, just sends someone to talk to the owner and get the lowest price possible. Once TNC members explain their purposes, they often find that people will donate their land.

TNC is certainly a major force in land preservation. In the last twenty-five years, the organization has saved over a million acres of different kinds of habitat. With so much to be done and so little time to do it, TNC is trying to save first the most ecologically important pieces of land that are in the most danger. In the prairie states, that means saving prairie. One big problem is that prairie land is expensive. To a farmer or a developer, it is like money in the bank, just waiting to be used.

TNC gets its money from private people, corporations, and foundations that donate it. Large corporations may give thousands of dollars, while regular members give ten dollars and students give five dollars. The group has enough money to locate and buy land, but nowhere near enough to take care of it forever. After the land is bought, TNC tries to transfer much of it to some other agency, such as a state conservation department or the U.S. Fish and Wildlife Service, for safekeeping. That way, the land

Prairie preserved. A sign proclaims this land set aside for scientific and educational use by The Nature Conservancy.

is saved, often at a much lower price than the government could have bought it, and TNC gets its money back.

The Nature Conservancy has been quietly buying prairies throughout the grassland states. The biggest purchase so far is a 7,600-acre tract in north central South Dakota. It cost $1.4 million. TNC plans to establish a biology station there, and several colleges are planning to study the area thoroughly. Whenever possible, TNC lands are used for scientific and educational purposes—as long as the land does not have to be harmed to achieve them.

TNC is not the only organization interested in saving prairie. Many grassland states have citizens' groups that will go to great lengths to get the job done. Sometimes The Nature Conservancy can help; other times the people themselves lead the effort.

Irene Herlocker, a retired chemist from Munster, Indiana, was taken by a friend to a "secret" bird-and-flower watching spot. It was a beautiful area of about 400 acres, rich with tall grass and flowers, that was completely surrounded by residential and industrial suburbs near Gary, Indiana. "I was stunned," she said. "I couldn't believe there was something so beautiful only ten minutes from my home." She bought a flower book and slowly began identifying plants.

Before long, she suspected that this was a true prairie remnant, saved by some quirk of chance where all the rest had been destroyed. She began contacting people. It turned out to be an area recognized by a handful of scientists as "the largest prairie of quality left in Indiana." But no one knew how to save it. Almost a fourth of the prairie had already been sold for an oil storage tank farm and destroyed.

Hoosier Prairie. Behind the trees you can see a petroleum storage tank. The tank farm is on land that once was prairie.

Since the land was in an excellent location for industry, it was worth at least a million dollars. The county had no money. The Indiana Division of Nature Preserves had no money. Even TNC could not handle a purchase of that size. Hoping that it could still be saved, Irene Herlocker continued contacting people. In 1969 she invited all of those who had shown an interest in it to a meeting at her home. They named the site the Hoosier Prairie and created the Hoosier Prairie Committee. Some of them were prairie experts, and they prepared a report that explained the special character of the tract. In 1970 they approached the owners and invited them to a luncheon and a tour of the land they owned. The owners refused to donate the land, but they did agree to hold it until a way could be found to save it.

In 1971 Congressman Edward Roush introduced a bill in the U.S. House of Representatives that would include the Hoosier Prairie in an expansion of the Indiana Dunes National Lakeshore. Even though the bill did not pass, the public became interested in the prairie, and Herlocker began speaking to organized groups about the tract and the committee's attempts to save it.

In 1973 The Nature Conservancy agreed to help acquire the Hoosier Prairie if it was included in the Indiana Dunes expansion bill. State Senator Ralph Potesta introduced a resolution urging the Indiana Department of Natural Resources to acquire the tract, and the department agreed to study the problem. Meanwhile, thirteen more acres were destroyed for an expansion to the tank farm.

In 1974 the Indiana Dunes bill, including Hoosier Prairie, was again introduced to Congress, but Congress thought that the state, and not the federal government, should buy it. A year later, the state of Indiana agreed to appropriate $1,000,000 for the Hoosier Prairie. TNC negotiated with the owners, and they settled on a purchase price of $900,000.

In 1976 the secretary of the interior agreed to contribute $450,000 toward the purchase of the land. Hoosier Prairie was at last included in the Indiana Dunes National Lakeshore, making it a national landmark on a par with Yosemite and the Grand Canyon. It is almost certain that the prairie would have been destroyed if Irene Herlocker had not decided to do something about it.

No matter who does the acquiring, buying a prairie is a beginning, not an end. If you were to buy a nice prairie, put a fence around it, and then walk away and leave it for ten or twenty years, you might be surprised when you return. In many tallgrass areas, you would come back to a young woods.

In the old days, the tallgrass prairies were kept in grass by wind, fire, and even bison (the bison rub against saplings and can actually push them over). But today, large wildfires rarely occur, the bison are few, and trees that serve as seed sources have been planted all over the prairie states.

To keep a modern prairie site in grass, someone has to be ready to manage it. The most common form of management is controlled burning. To most people, burning a park seems crazy, because burning has been associated with destruction. But if a management crew knows what they are doing, they can use fire to keep a prairie healthy.

Fire kills most woody plants, especially when they are small. If the area is burned in the spring before hot weather, the fire will also kill European weeds because

Using fire for prairie management requires skill in knowing what and when to burn and how to do it safely.

the weeds sprout earlier in the year than most of the prairie plants. Fire also prevents an accumulation of dead plant parts from smothering the young prairie plants.

Fire is necessary, but dangerous, and should be used only by trained crews. A fire at the wrong time or too frequent burning can harm some prairie species. Management crews are experienced at using fire breaks to control the flames. They burn only after getting permission from fire and police departments. In some areas they also need permission from pollution control agencies because of the smoke that goes into the air. The management of a prairie is sometimes a big job. But without it, all the effort to preserve a site could be for nothing.

10.

MAKE YOUR OWN PRAIRIE

It has recently become obvious that all of the eastern prairies that can be saved have been saved. There just isn't much more tallgrass prairie left. In the western plains there are still some shortgrass prairies, but many of them are in bad shape because of overgrazing. In such situations, people are turning to "prairie restoration"; they are rebuilding damaged prairie or even starting from scratch. "People realize that something has fallen apart, and they're finding a great challenge in trying to put it back together again," says Jim Zimmerman, a restoration expert at the University of Wisconsin Arboretum.[25]

Sometimes groups want to restore a prairie so there will be one where people can get to it and see it. They put a prairie right where they want it. Their reasoning is that if people could see even a dim version of what the prairies once were, then they would surely become interested in the real thing.

There's one big problem—restoring a prairie to *exactly* the way it was is impossible. Even an approximation is expensive, slow, and difficult. But thanks to the hard work done by several arboretums, universities, and devoted friends of the prairie, we are learning how to go about it as best we can.

Suppose you are standing before a plowed field. There is absolutely no trace of prairie on it. How should you go about building a prairie?

The first step is to decide what kind of a prairie will grow on the site. Is the field sand or clay? Is the soil dry or wet? Is it in a tallgrass or shortgrass area? Exactly which plants you choose to put in is important because plants are adapted to grow in different situations.

One way to get started would be to find a prairie and steal plants from it, but that would be disturbing the master copy. No fair! Sometimes, you can rescue plants from a construction site by digging them up before the bulldozers find them. Unfortunately, such plants are growing on root stalks that may be many years old, and they have spent years adapting to their site. When you move them, they may never get used to the new place. They will hang on for a few years and then give up.

The best way to start prairie plants is from seed. Sometimes garden companies carry a few varieties of prairie flowers, but if you compare the plants to the wild ones, they often look a bit different. That is because the seed companies may have gotten their original seed stock from a prairie far from yours. Also, the garden companies may be taking seed only from the prettiest flowers,

Big bluestem (left) and blazing star (right) will grow from the seeds you collect.

rather than the tough, rangy ones that might do better in your prairie.

The experts find prairies growing on sites similar to those they want to restore and pick some of the seeds. They look for the seeds in places that are not customarily plowed, such as railroad right-of-ways, roadside ditches, and even pioneer cemeteries. Gathering the seeds must be done throughout the growing season because the plants ripen their seeds at different times. Again, it would not be fair to take all the seeds of one kind of plant. To get

Prairie clover (left) and pasque flower (right) transplant easily.

a natural-looking prairie, however, it is important to obtain a few seeds from many different kinds of plants.

The seeds have natural timers that tell them when to sprout. So they do not disturb these timers, restorationists put the seeds through a winter, either by storing them outside in paper sacks or in the refrigerator with moist sand. If they are put in a place that is too dry, such as inside a heated house, they will usually die.

Spring is planting time. Some people scatter the seeds outside right away, while others start them in greenhouses so they get a jump on the weeds. European weeds are always a problem at first; they are "professionals" at growing on plowed land. The prairie plants, though, only grow from seeds that land on hard ground or from shoots off a parent plant. As Jim Wilson, a prairie restorationist puts it, "The first year, chances are you'll have a weed patch. If you don't get disgusted and plow it up, the second year you'll probably have a miracle."[26]

Prairie plants are slow growers but tough. They spend the whole first year pushing roots down as far as possible. A one-inch bluestem seedling may have roots a foot deep. Most of the European weeds are annuals; that is, they start growing from seed every year. As the years go by, the deep-rooted, prairie plants have more and more of an advantage. A good spring burn every few years gives them even more of a jump. In five years prairie plants should be growing and reproducing freely.

Eventually, if you keep working on it, your site should look much as it did in the old days. "Eventually," according to the experts, means 100 years, or 300 years, or 500 years, depending on which expert you talk to. It may be impossible to bring back the old days—bison and prairie dogs are just not welcome in most city parks —but in a small way it is possible to bring back a hint of the past glory.

The best restorations have been done by professionals, and it has taken them years. The staff at the University of Wisconsin Arboretum has been working since 1936 to restore 100 acres of prairie with about 300 kinds of flowers and 25 kinds of grass. The Morton Arboretum at Lisle, Illinois, has spent thousands of dollars to re-establish about 120 kinds of prairie plants on 10 acres near Chicago. These are really incredible projects.

Prairie restoration is for all ages. These children are collecting blazing star seeds to be planted at the Woodlake Nature Center.

Achieving the desired diversity is what takes the most time. If you accept a simpler prairie, at least as a start, the task is greatly reduced. Peter Schram at Knox College has gotten thirty kinds of flowers and six kinds of grasses growing in a nice-looking prairie in five years. But he had the help of college students, who put in hours of seed gathering, sorting, planting, weeding, and maintenance.

A less ambitious prairie project is possible for schools and small nature centers. At Wood Lake Nature Center in Richfield, Minnesota, schoolchildren and neighbors helped gather seeds at nearby prairie remnants. Students also donated money that was used to buy some seeds. Volunteers sorted and labeled the seeds. In the spring, children helped sow the seeds and transplant seedlings. They also spread a mulch of prairie hay over the sandy soil. Summer volunteers helped with weeding. Every season there is something to be done on the ongoing prairie project. Every year the project is expanded to cover a little more land.

Schools in prairie states can easily recreate a small patch of "simplified" prairie on their grounds. A person who can help in finding seeds and give advice on caring for them may be contacted by calling nature centers, state and federal agencies, and even local garden clubs. Prairie restoration has become such a growing movement that companies have been formed to help with projects. Such businesses will act as consultants or do the whole project themselves.

Jim Wilson, who made a business of selling the seeds of prairie plants, has a theory about the new interest in prairie restoration:

> The whole country is gripped in a feeling of apprehension and uncertainty and anxiety about the future. People seem to long for something that will give them a sense of security and continuity and permanence, and somehow these prairie grasses and flowers seem to do it. The darn things seem to reassure people somehow. They represent permanence and persistence in the face of danger . . . persisting things you know.[27]

The best thing about restoration is that you can put a prairie where the people are. But the problem with restoration sites is that all the good ones are small. Establishing a big prairie that looks authentic would not be economically possible. The only hope for a really big tract of prairie is to find one to preserve.

11.

A PRAIRIE NATIONAL PARK

All of the preservation and restoration attempts we have discussed so far are tiny in comparison with a prairie national park. It should be big—so big that you could walk all day without seeing a sign that people lived nearby. At least sixty thousand acres would be a good size.

In 1961, after five years of study, the National Park Service proposed a 57,000-acre prairie park near Manhattan, Kansas. This area has the largest remaining tract of unplowed tallgrass prairie in the United States. It had escaped the plow because the soil is shallow and underlain by flinty rock. The rolling country of the Flint Hills is poor cropland, but excellent for grazing. In many places, cattle ranchers have done an excellent job of

This cross section of the Flint Hills prairie shows why it is poor cropland.

preventing overgrazing, and the prairie is still beautiful.

The 1961 proposal was bitterly opposed by the ranchers, who wanted to stay on the land they owned. Since there was little public support, the proposal was dropped and nearly forgotten.

The National Park Service (NPS), however, couldn't forget. It has a responsibility to conserve typical parts of the nation's major natural habitats. The NPS had done well in preserving samples of such habitats as the Everglades in Florida, the Great Smoky Mountains in Tennessee and North Carolina, and the Olympic rain forests in the state of Washington. But nowhere did we have a national park to preserve prairie, the habitat that once covered one-third of the United States.

In 1971, the NPS recommended that the Flint Hills proposal be reconsidered. This time the recommendation stated that only part of the national park would be publicly owned. The rest could be privately owned under certain restrictions, one of which was that no plowing would be allowed.

Also in 1971, Senator James Pearson and Congressman Larry Winn, Jr., of Kansas, introduced bills in Congress calling for the creation of a sixty thousand-acre prairie park in the Flint Hills. It had to be that large, they said, because that much land is necessary to show the vastness and openness of the prairie as it once was. Sixty thousand acres is also enough land to support bison in a natural setting. The other Kansas delegates were not in favor of the bills. Without strong support from Kansans. Congress remained unmoved, and no action was taken. It seemed that there was nothing to be done.

Outside the halls of Congress, there were many people who had been interested in a prairie park for a long time, and they were not about to give up. It took a while to get things organized, but by 1973 they had banded together and created "Save the Tallgrass Prairie, Inc." (STP). Their purpose was to alert Kansas and the nation to the danger the prairie was in. They wanted a tallgrass prairie national park in the Flint Hills.

Shortly after STP was formed in 1973, a Kansas congressional delegation asked the National Park Service to study once more the possibility of a national park in Kansas. In 1975, the NPS published the results of its study, which recommended three Kansas areas to be "further evaluated."

As the National Park Service studied different ideas for managing these areas, the members of Save the Tallgrass Prairie stepped up their campaign to find support for a wild prairie park. The Flint Hills ranchers who

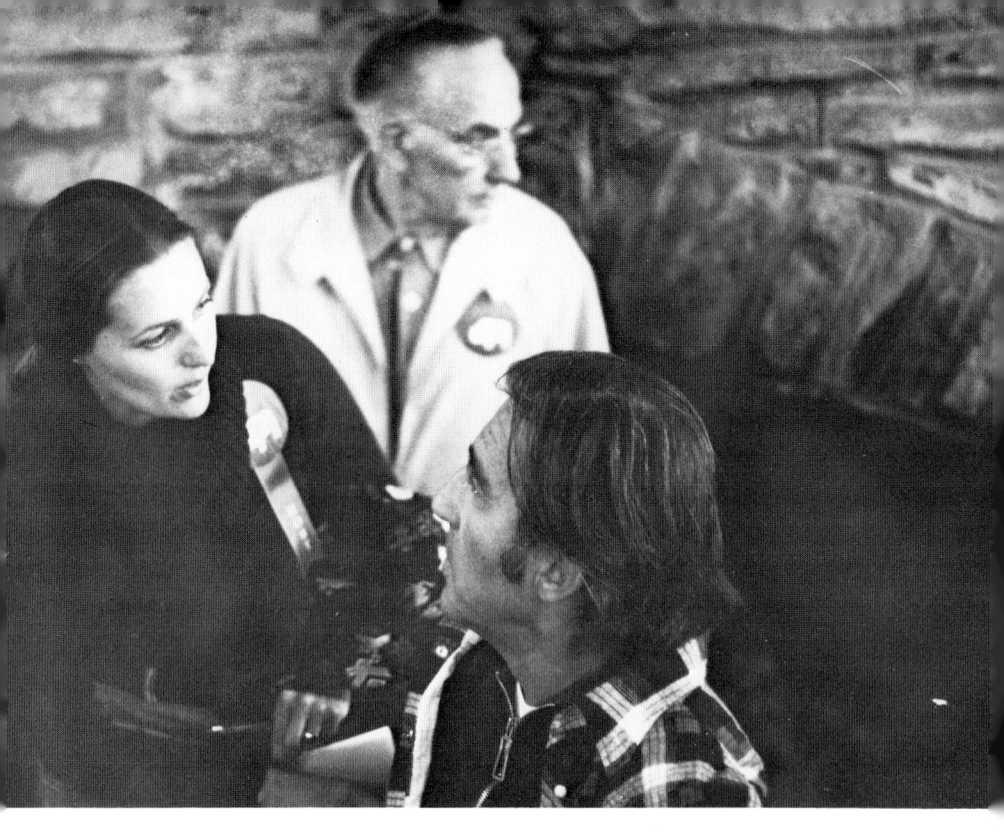

Elaine Shea, Director of STP, talks with Stewart Udall, former Secretary of the Interior. Dr. E. Raymond Hall, one of the founders of the organization, is in the background.

opposed the park also formed an organization, the Kansas Grassroots Association (KGA). Up and down the state of Kansas the arguments went on, as each group pleaded for its cause.

The federal government already owns enough Kansas land to make a park, the KGA said. Why destroy healthy ranches needlessly? To this, STP replied that the federal land in Kansas is not suitable for a prairie park. The only two federal sites large enough are Fort Riley and the Cimmaron National Grasslands. The army is not willing to give up Fort Riley, and the Cimmaron grasslands have been badly abused by plowing and overgrazing.

Another point the ranchers brought up was that in a time of high beef prices and food shortages, it is unwise to take land out of beef production. The prairie people's answer was that the number of cattle supported on sixty thousand acres is equal to only .001 of the states's beef production. Surely, they said, preserving the last large piece of tallgrass prairie in the U.S. is worth that.

The Flint Hills are still beautiful prairie. Isn't that because we have taken care of them so well? the ranchers asked. Don't you think we will continue the good management practices that have worked so well before? But such management is for the good of your cattle, the prairie people said. We want the prairie made safe for bison, elk, and all the wild creatures that belong there. Suppose you had to make a choice between doing something to the land that would be good for raising cattle and not doing it because it would harm the wild creatures. What would you decide? Besides, who can say that those who own the land after you will take as good care of it. Fifty years from now it might be sold to real estate developers who would build houses on it.

Both sides fear that a national park would attract tourist traps that would cheapen the surrounding countryside. There are several ways this could be prevented. One is that the surrounding ranchers could agree not to sell land to developers. In addition, the county could zone the land so it could not be developed. Or the federal government could buy "scenic easements" to guarantee that the surrounding area would stay beautiful.

For many Kansans, the core of the issue is the role of the federal government. Many people feel that the federal government should not take private citizens' land away from them. Other people feel that the federal government acts for everyone, to do things in the name of the whole country. Sometimes one hundred people must be inconvenienced for the good of all the other people in the country. What do you think about this?

Both groups worked hard to bring the issue before the public. The people of Kansas and their lawmakers began to take notice—and take sides.

In April 1975, a terrific blow was dealt to STP. The Kansas senate passed a resolution that urged Congress to reject a bill proposing the park. Congressman Winn ignored the resolution. Three months later he introduced another, stronger bill in Congress. This time the bill had twenty-one cosponsors—a sign that the bill was backed by other representatives. But the bill was locked up in the House Interior and Insular Affairs Committee, and no action was taken.

It became clear that the prairie park bill had a powerful enemy on the committee. He was Congressman Joe Skubitz, a representative from Kansas whose district contained one of the proposed sites. As the ranking Republican member, he was in a good position to block the proposal each time it came up. This was exactly what the ranchers who elected him had asked him to do.

The future of the park began to look brighter with the coming of the Bicentennial. A new federal tax law that was passed in 1976 removed one of the strongest arguments against the park. It stated that the federal government would pay local governments for the tax money they lost on land that was set aside for national parks. The prairie people cheered. In August 1976, the prairie issue gained national publicity when it was discussed on the "Robert MacNeil Report," a thirty-minute television program aired by the Public Broadcasting Service. Not long afterwards, STP was asked to put on their own television show by the Kansas City public television station. A letter stating their hopes for a tallgrass prairie national park was placed in a Bicentennial time capsule and buried for the future.

The Bicentennial publicity gave a needed boost to the cause. By 1977, STP had gathered more than forty thousand names on petitions and had members in forty-three states. The National Sierra Club considered the creation of a prairie national park to be "top priority." It was also one of the top four priorities of another group, Friends of the Earth. Other environmental organizations such as the National Audubon Society, The Nature Conservancy, and the Wilderness Society also backed the establishment of a prairie park.

Widespread support for the park now made it a more popular political issue. On February 9, 1977, when the Kansas legislature considered another resolution opposing the park, it was killed in committee. Later in the same month, Congressman Skubitz announced that he would not run for re-election in 1978. The fact that he would no longer be on the House Internal and Insular Affairs Committee the next time a bill proposing the park came before it might give the bill a better chance.

In September 1977 Congressman Winn introduced a new bill that he hoped would be acceptable to the Flint Hills ranchers as well as to the prairie supporters. Unlike the previous bills, this one allowed for a much larger area—187,000 acres—to be divided into two parts. About half of the tract would be called the Tallgrass Prairie National Park, while the other half would be the Tallgrass Prairie National Preserve. Owners of land in the preserve would keep certain rights to it. For example, they would have a right to the oil, natural gas, and mineral deposits that have been found there. Those who sold their land for the park would have no further control over it, but the bill takes their problems into account. Once they sold their land to the government, they would have six years to find a new ranch. If they wished, they could stay in their homes for twenty-five years or the rest of their lives. But eventually all the land in the park itself would belong to the people of the United States. Another fear, that of ugly tourist traps around the park, was also put to rest. A combination of zoning restrictions and scenic easements would make sure that everything one could see from the park and the preserve would be kept scenic.

The bill is now on its way. But before it can become law, however, it must be passed by the House and the Senate and signed by the president. There are many steps along the way, and it could be stopped at any one of them.

Unfortunately, time is running out. The Flint Hills are no longer safe as a "bank" of tallgrass prairie. In 1974-1975, several thousand acres of virgin prairie in the Flint Hills were plowed and planted with fescue and bromegrass, plants not typical of the area. These grasses produce more foliage in the spring and fall than the regular tall grasses. Many Flint Hills ranchers opposed the plowing experiment, but if it provides better grazing for their cattle and higher profits, property owners in the Flint Hills will have a hard choice to make.

New methods of raising cattle are bound to have an effect on the Flint Hills prairie, too. Ten years ago, steers grazed there only in the summer. Most of the ranchers burned the grass in the spring to keep out woody

The Flint Hills of Kansas is the only place remaining with large, unbroken vistas like this that recall the early days of our nation.

plants and encourage healthy grass growth. Today, the pattern has changed from summer grazing by steers to yearlong cropping by cows and calves as well. Thus the grass is kept short over the winter. In the spring there is not enough fuel left to carry a fire, and the woody plants that cattle do not eat are invading the prairie.

The Flint Hills prairie is becoming less and less natural. Soon it may no longer be a sample of what the pioneers saw. It is up to everyone in the country, not just Kansans, to decide whether there will be a prairie national park. If we want a park, we have to make one now.

As Lawrence Wagner, a man in favor of the park, wrote, "In the event that the Tallgrass Prairie National Park becomes a reality, no one likely will remember those persons who were responsible. If we do *not* succeed in our efforts, we will be remembered as the generation that had the last clear chance to preserve this priceless heritage and that we failed. I would rather not be remembered than to be so remembered."[28] Although Wagner was speaking about a particular issue, his thoughts apply to all of us and all of the prairie that is left.

Everyone has heard of people who stand by and do not help when they are needed. Perhaps they want to avoid the extra work, but is it worth it? How do you think Irene Herlocker felt when her Hoosier Prairie was recognized as a National Landmark? Do you think she thought it was worth the work? Maybe in twenty years few people will remember that it was she who saved the Hoosier Prairie. But if the last prairies are destroyed in our lifetime, our descendants will remember us as the people who stood by and watched. We are the ones, the people in control. How do you want to be remembered?

NOTES

1. George Catlin, *Letters and Notes on the Manners, Customs, and Conditions of North American Indians* (New York: Dover Publications, 1973), p. 17.
2. *Audubon Magazine,* July 1972, p. 18.
3. John G. Neihardt, *Black Elk Speaks* (New York: Morrow Inc., 1932) p. 1.
4. Reginald and Gladys Laubin, *The Indian Tipi* (Norman: University of Oklahoma, 1957), p. 4.
5. Luther Standing Bear, *My People the Sioux* (Boston and New York: Houghton Mifflin Co., 1928), p. 14.
6. George Catlin, *Letter and Notes on the North American Indians,* ed. M. Mooney (New York: Clarkson Potter, Inc., 1975), p. 169.
7. Luther Standing Bear, *My People the Sioux* (Boston and New York: Houghton Mifflin Co., 1928), p. 10.
8. Margot Astrov, *American Indian Prose and Poetry* (New York: Capricorn Books, 1946), p. 85.
9. Waldo Wedel, *Prehistoric Man on the Great Plains* (Norman: University of Oklahoma Press, 1961), p. 201.
10. Ibid., p. 278.
11. Ibid., p. 80.
12. Edmund and Martha Bray, *Joseph N. Nicollet on the Plains and Prairies* (St. Paul: Minnesota Historical Society, 1976), p. 52.
13. Thomas E. Mails, *The Mystic Warriors of the Plains* (New York: Doubleday and Co., 1972), p. 11.
14. Ibid.
15. *Natural History Magazine,* May 1977, p. 53.
16. Ibid., p. 52.

17. *Audubon Magazine,* July 1972, p. 18.
18. David F. Costello, *The Prairie World* (New York: Thomas Y. Crowell Co., 1969), p. 96.
19. Faith McNulty, *Must They Die?* (New York: Doubleday and Co., 1971), p. 58.
20. Ibid., p. 49.
21. *The Nature Conservancy News,* Winter 1977, p. 12.
22. *Ecosphere,* 2 (no. 1): June 1971.
23. *Audubon Magazine,* Nov. 1972, p. 18.
24. Torkel Korling, *The Prairie—Swell and Swale* (Dundee, Illinois: Torkel Korling, 1972), p. 10.
25. *Smithsonian,* July 1975, p. 61.
26. Ibid., p. 63.
27. Ibid.
28. Kansas Senate *Hearings,* March 27, 1975.

GLOSSARY

carnivore—a meat-eating animal
community—all of the living things in an area taken together
diversity—variety; used here to describe complex ecosystems like virgin prairie as opposed to a monotonous area like a cornfield
dormant—inactive; used here to describe plants that stop growing during certain times of the year
ecosystem—the natural community plus the non-living things and the way they interact. Ecosystems can be very large, like the planet Earth, or small, like a rotting log
habitat—the place where an animal lives; for example, the habitat of whales is in the ocean while the habitat of prairie dogs is short grass prairie
herbicide—a chemical that kills plants
herbivore—an animal that eats plants
indicator plant—a plant that is a clue to something about the ecosystem. For example, cactus plants indicate low rainfall
mammal—a warm-blooded animal that nourishes its young with its milk
nomad—a person who has no fixed home, but wanders from place to place as a way of life
pollinate—to put pollen grains (male parts of a flower) on the stigma (female part of a flower); this results in the formation of seeds
predator—an animal that captures and eats other animals
prey—an animal eaten by another animal
rodents—gnawing mammals such as mice, squirrels, and beavers
scavenger—an animal that eats dead things

BIBLIOGRAPHY

Allen, Durward L. *The Life of Prairies and Plains.* New York: McGraw-Hill, 1967.
Costello, David F. *The Prairie World.* New York: Thomas Y. Crowell Co., 1969.
Johnson, J. and J. Nichols. *Plants of South Dakota Grasslands.* Bull. 566. Agricultural Experiment Station, Brookings, South Dakota, 1970.
Korling, Torkel. *The Prairie—Swell and Swale.* Dundee, Illinois: Torkel Korling, 1972.
Pohl, R. *How to Know the Grasses.* Dubuque: Wm. C. Brown Co., 1953.
Peterson, Roger Tory, editor, *The Peterson Field Guide Series.* Boston: Houghton Mifflin Co.
Rock, Harold W. *Prairie Propagation Handbook.* Milwaukee: Boerner Botanical Gardens, 1971.

The Nature Conservancy has control of more prairieland than any other organization. To find out about this group, write: The Nature Conservancy, 1800 North Kent Street, Arlington, Virginia, 22209.
 The National Park Service will send you a state-by-state inventory of 48,000 parks, some of which have prairie. Write: National Park Service, U.S. Dept. of the Interior, Washington, D.C., 20240. For more information about the prospect of a prairie national park, write to Save the Tallgrass Prairie, Inc., 4101 W. 54th Terrace, Shawnee Mission, Kansas, 66205.

DISCARD